TIME TO TOUGHEN UP

Develop Immense Inner Strength And Confidence Overcome Challenges And Achieve Your Goals

MARK LLEWHELLIN

Book 10 in the
Mark Llewhellin
Success and Happiness Series

DEDICATION

To the love of my life, my little miracle, Léon James Llewhellin, who I love more than anyone in the world. You are kind, thoughtful, well balanced and you are already achieving great things in your life because of your mental toughness.

Words cannot describe how much I love you and how proud I am of the person you are.

To you the reader
LIFE CAN BE TOUGH, BUT YOU ARE TOUGHER!

GET TWO OF MARK'S BOOKS FOR FREE

Join Mark's team for information on new books along with special offers and pick up a FREE copy of Mark's 5 star reviewed books:

'The Underdog' and 'Delusions Of Grandeur.'

Details can be found at the end of this book.

"Tough times never last, but tough people do."

– Robert H. Schuller

TABLE OF CONTENTS

CHAPTER 1

YOU'RE NOT GOING TO BREAK ME

"My dad used to beat the living daylights out of me. You can't let that kind of thing affect you in any way, because then you're carrying that weight all the way through life. You can't think about it too deeply because it would drive you fucking mad."

– Noel Gallagher

Time To Toughen Up

The sergeant clenched his fist and raised his hand high above his head, and, with a hammer-like blow, he smashed his fist down onto my fingers as hard as he could!

As his knuckles connected, I felt the pain shooting through my fingers. It was the first time that I had come across a bully with such an age gap. Sergeant Goddard was in his 30s and I was a 16-year-old kid. I had joined the army and was away from home in a new environment, just trying to make something of my life.

And the reason he smashed his fist into my hand? He was checking for dirt on the fingernails of the recruits after we had showered. He would criticise often and praise rarely.

Goddard hated me with a passion. He hated that I wanted to be somebody, and he was determined that he was going to squash my dreams. I wasn't the only kid he hit or gave shit to. He did it to everybody in the troop that didn't kiss his arse or come up to his impossible fucked-up standards.

He didn't like anything about me. Whenever he shouted at me, hit me, humiliated me, or put doubts into my young head about my abilities, I only had one thought in my mind,

"Fuck you, you're not going to break me!"

As far as I was concerned, he was just another dick that I had to get past to achieve my dreams.

You're going to come across a lot of dicks in your life.

Some people will:

- Belittle you.
- Talk shit about you behind your back.
- Not help you when you've helped them.
- Screw you over.
- Try to bully you.
- Laugh at your dreams.

And

- Try to hold you back.

But it's not just other people that you'll have to toughen up for. There are a lot of things that will happen to you that are simply not fair, and you don't deserve them, but they will come into your life, that's just the game. The game may not be fair, and it can be brutal, but that's the way it is.

To get through this sometimes-brutal life, we all have to toughen up whether we like it or not. This book will give you the strength and the information you need to become a stronger person and develop immense mental toughness.

The greatest gift you can have is mental toughness. Mental strength beats anything and everything.

Power doesn't beat it, recognition doesn't beat it, awards and achievements don't beat it and money doesn't beat it. Forget about all the Christmas presents you received when you were a child, they don't compare. Even if you won the lottery, nothing but NOTHING beats having immense mental strength!

When you are strong mentally, you can endure anything that is thrown at you. It's a power that can make you feel almost invincible!

Think about the movies you've watched when there is a hero involved. That hero has a journey that he or she must take. All sorts of things can happen to that hero. They can lose all of their money, their relationships can crumble, people close to them get hurt or die, but, with a bit of time and a bit of help, they get through it.

There is one common denominator about all of our heroes in real life or in the movies, they are all mentally strong!

Whether it's Russell Crow's gladiator character slicing and dicing people and shouting, "Are you not entertained?" Or the D.C. and Marvel superheroes saving the world.

Heroes are strong but can also feel weak and have doubts. They sometimes lose and get knocked back, and that's when they know it's time to toughen up!

When they toughen up, they take on the challenges they must face and at the end of the battle, they come through victorious!

Some people are born mentally tougher than others, however mental toughness can also be learned. My goal with this book is to help you develop more mental toughness and help you overcome the many battles that you will have to face.

Never forget, you're a warrior, you're a champion, you are a winner, and nothing and no one can break you! You are stronger than any challenges you face.

So, whenever you get hurt by people or knocked back in life, it's time to toughen up!

CHAPTER 2

LORD OF TOUGHNESS

"Show me someone who has done something worthwhile, and I'll show you someone who has overcome adversity."

– Lou Holtz

On 3rd January 1890, a baby boy called John was born in South Africa.

When John was only three years old, his father died; this was devastating to the entire family. His mother wasn't sure what was best for John and his younger brother Hilary but decided that moving to England would be the best thing for all of them.

As he went through his childhood, John would immerse himself in reading books. It was common for people to read the works of Shakespeare, but Shakespeare didn't appeal to John. He lost himself in fantasy books about Norse gods such as Odin and Thor and also loved reading fairy-tale books.

He wrote his first story called, 'The Green Great Dragon,' when he was still a child.

At age seven, John took a test to get into school, which he

failed at first but later passed. Finances were tight for his family, so he had to walk four miles to school every day. Things were looking up for John and he was optimistic about life. Little did he know, tragedy was about to strike his family once again.

John's mum was diagnosed with diabetes and she gradually deteriorated. On 14th November 1904 John's mum died. This was devastating to both John and his brother! The woman they loved more than anyone in the world was now gone from their lives. He was only 14 years old.

John and his brother were now orphans. Fortunately, a half Welsh, half Spanish Catholic priest stepped in and raised both John and his brother Hilary. Father Francis Xavier Morgan was a friend of John's mother and cared for her while she was dying. Father Morgan's influence on John would have a profound effect on both his life and his writing.

When John was 16, he dated a 19-year-old girl by the name of Edith, and they fell in love. However, Father Morgan didn't approve of their relationship, so the relationship ended. This was another blow for John.

He lost himself in his schoolwork and got a scholarship to Oxford University. John had gone from failing academically to getting into one of the most prestigious universities in the world. It was at Oxford where he pursued his study of linguistics and studied both Welsh and Finnish.

John soon got to an age where Father Morgan was no longer his legal guardian, so he was keen to spark up the relationship again with Edith. He sent her a letter and asked when they could meet up. Edith replied, however, it wasn't the letter that John was hoping for. She was now engaged to another man. John was incredibly upset and rushed to Edith to persuade her not to get married. By the end of the day, she broke off her engagement and committed herself back to John.

In 1914 the world plunged into darkness when World War I started. John continued studying, and in 1915, he graduated from Oxford with first-class honours. One year later he enlisted in the Lancaster Fusiliers and took a position as a signals officer in the British Army.

In the summer of 1916, John fought in the Battle of the Somme and experienced the horrors of World War I. He lost two close friends. By 1918, all but one of John's friends was dead! To add to the hardships he'd already been through while abroad, John picked up trench fever and was sick on and off for the next two years.

Life wasn't all darkness for John. Shortly after he came

back to England, he became a professor at the University of Leeds and Edith gave birth to their first of four children. Then, in 1922, John's first academic book was published, it was called, 'A Middle English Vocabulary.'

After his time at Leeds, John returned to Oxford to teach. Then, one day, when he was marking his student's papers, he noticed there was a blank page on the student's paper. John was always daydreaming and kept staring at the blank page in front of him. As he looked at the blank page, with pencil in hand, he slowly and carefully wrote 10 words down.

'In a hole in the ground there lived a hobbit.'

From those first 10 words, John continued writing. 95,365 words later, he had completed a novel.

When he started writing the book, it was mainly for his own satisfaction, and he didn't think that anyone else would be interested in it. He also thought people would think he was wasting his time. However, John carried on writing, but when he finished it, he wouldn't give it to a literary professional to edit. This isn't standard practice. However, he knew he needed expert advice to see if the book was any good. But rather than ask anybody in the publishing world to review his book, he paid his son to read it. John wanted to see if his son liked it because he believed children were the best judges of fantasy books.

It turned out that his son loved it! This encouraged John, so he continued writing more books.

As you may have guessed by now from the hobbit reference, John is none other than John Ronald Reuel Tolkien, AKA – J. R. R. Tolkien, author of The Hobbit and The Lord of the Rings.

And the rest, as they say, is history.

Although Tolkien didn't like his books being compared to events such as World War I or World War II, his books carried many of the same themes in life, such as

- Courage.
- Love.
- Teamwork.
- Accepting different cultures.
- Carrying on when all hope seems lost.

John lost himself in myth and fantasy. It was escapism from some of the harsh realities of life.

Maybe your reality isn't the fantasy world that you want. You dream of a better life for yourself. One thing for certain is, if you want to live the life of the hero or heroine, you've got to be mentally tough, just like many of the characters in John Tolkien's books.

In his books, there is always conflict, whether it's internal conflict or external conflict. In one part of the book the heroes and heroines can fight orcs or dragons, and in another part of the book, they can be alone but are suffering from self-doubt and fear. It can be the same for us in real life too.

Our physical well-being may not be in harm's way, but there will be times for each and every one of us where we'll be in the comfort of our own homes and we'll question our ability to do something.

This is normal for all human beings. It's important to take comfort in the knowledge that you are not alone when negative thoughts come into your mind.

One of Tolkien's friends was Clive Staples Lewis, otherwise known as C. S. Lewis, famous for writing the Lion, the Witch and the Wardrobe and the Chronicles of Narnia seven book series. C. S. Lewis and J. R. R. Tolkien would always encourage each other about the books they were writing, and they inspired one another. They even pushed each other out of their comfort zones.

In Tolkien's books, his characters are also taken out of

their comfort zone. Apart from the army of the dead. They were already dead, so to be fair, they didn't have much to lose.

On a more serious note, you can be inspired to go out of your comfort zone from a friend, from a book, from a movie or a song. It's highly unlikely that you're going to face the challenges that the heroes in Tolkien's books faced, so what have you got to lose?

J. R. R. Tolkien went through the fire of life when he lost his parents. He had a choice to make from an early age. Either he could

1. Give up and let those two incidents destroy the rest of his life.
   or
2. He could toughen up and make the most of what he had.

He chose option 2 and so can you!

CHAPTER 3

THE BLAME GAME

"As long as you blame others for the reason you aren't where you want to be, you will always be a failure."
– Erin Cummings

Many people are quick to blame their upbringing, their race, religion, colour, sex and whatever else they can for their challenges in life. They scream for attention and claim to be a victim. These days people are also quick to blame their education, their bosses, or their country's leaders for their own failures. It's always someone else's fault. Many people love to throw around blame and are reluctant to take responsibility for their own shortcomings. But if we sit there complaining all the time, all we do is cause self-inflicted mental health issues.

A great example of throwing around blame is when people try to sue places like McDonald's for making them fat. They blame McDonald's for causing their medical issues. In reality, the type of food that someone eats is the responsibility of the individual. They are the ones that 'chose' to eat what they put in their mouth.

Sometimes it's not your fault when you fail. If you're an athlete, you can get injured through no fault of your own.

That is something that can be out of your hands and is a valid reason.

When my friend Daz Crane was on the Commando Course doing a death jump, through no fault of his own he broke his ankle. The death jump is when you throw yourself off a rock face while attached to a rope with your hands on your head. It's to prove you have courage, and the test is also designed to encourage you to trust in your equipment and your teammate.

At the bottom of the rock face is a brake man or brake woman who is supposed to pull the rope tight just before you hit the ground. Pulling the rope puts the brakes on and stops you from hitting the ground. Unfortunately for Daz, the instructor at the bottom pulled the rope too late and Daz broke his ankle.

He failed that Commando Course because somebody didn't do the job that they were supposed to do. I guess perhaps it was half Daz's fault for jumping off the rock face, but it's rare that somebody hits the bottom. Of course, Daz was pissed off, but he didn't complain and give up. He put on his big boy pants, went back when the injury had healed, and passed the course.

Winners don't play the victim role!

And when I talk about winners, I'm not talking about people who achieve a lot of things like awards, money or recognition. We've all seen some celebrities feeling sorry for themselves when they've got nothing to complain about. When I say winners, I mean people who don't bitch about their circumstances or what someone has done to them, they accept their situation and power on!

If you live in a rich country like Great Britain, Canada, America or another wealthy country, you have a tremendous advantage in life.

And if you've been healthy for most of your life and have medical support in your country, then you've also got a massive advantage over billions of other people.

People who have parents that are well-connected or financially well off can also have a tremendous advantage over others. However, having these things doesn't automatically make you a winner.

The real winners in life:

- Don't complain all the time.
- Are optimistic.
- Know what they want.
- Think big.
- Are determined.

- Face their fears.
- Push themselves past their comfort zone.
- Are focused.
- Take massive action towards their goals.
- Are kind.
- Focus on solutions, not problems.
- Are persistent.
- Go the extra mile to help other people.
- And they are grateful every single day for what they have, and who they have in their life.

In the British comedy sketch about Kevin and Perry, ungrateful and moody teenager Kevin blames his parents for not having the perfect life. However, in reality, Kevin has an incredible life and has many of life's creature comforts. He just doesn't see it.

How many people do you know like this?

Do you know people who have the world at their feet but they're complaining and saying what they've got isn't enough? The irony of this is, they're not moving closer towards happiness or being a winner, they're moving further away from being happy. This is because they're not grateful for what they already have.

At the end of one Kevin and Perry sketch, Kevin's father says to Kevin's mother, "Don't worry darling it's only a phase, it will only last 4 to 5 years."

This may be true with some teenagers, but there are teenagers that bring that victim mentality with them into adulthood and have it throughout their entire lives. The truth is you can act like a victim at any age. To act like a victim all the way through your life is to live the life of the snowflake.

Of course, it's not fair or correct to say that all teenagers act like this. Some teenagers are well behaved and very strong mentally. My son Léon for example, is only 11 and is a well-balanced, kind and mentally strong child. At the time of writing I'm proud to say that he just won his junior school sprint race and his cross-country race. He also picked up the award for Best Athlete, and a certificate for being the top student in his year at drama.

I was extremely fortunate to have such a kind child and I will claim some credit for that. He's only been given a handful of 'time outs' in his life. Léon learned from his mistakes and decided that being put on timeout was a waste of his time. He adjusted his behaviour, and, as a result, he gets more of the things he wants and does more of the things he enjoys.

However, having worked with children that have special needs, autism and learning difficulties, I can also say with confidence, there are many great parents who have children that can be extremely challenging. Some children have specific psychological challenges, so there are different ways to get the best out of each individual child. But that is a whole series of books in itself.

In a Psychology Today article, Susan Krauss Whitbourne Ph.D. wrote an article called 'Five Reasons We Play The Blame Game.'

They are:

- Blame is an excellent defence mechanism. Blame helps you preserve your sense of self-esteem by avoiding awareness of your own flaws or failings.

- Blame is a tool we use when we are in attack mode. This falls into the category of destructive conflict resolution method where we try to hurt other people.

- We are not very good at figuring out the causes of other people's behaviour, or even our own.

- It's easier to blame someone else than to accept responsibility. There is less effort involved in recognising your contributions to a bad situation than accepting the fact that you're actually at fault.

- People lie. It's easy to lie and blame someone else even though you know you're at fault.

Susan concludes the article by saying, "The more often you play the blame game, the more you lose."

Ultimately, playing the blame game is a sign of weakness. If somebody has messed up, it may piss you off initially. However, to keep that blame and hatred for them within yourself is poisonous to your soul and destroys your own happiness in life.

And if you blame yourself for messing up, then take responsibility for screwing up, but don't dwell on it. We all mess up, and that's just part of life. What's important is that we learn from our mistakes and stay optimistic about our future.

CHAPTER 4

WHEN PEOPLE YOU'VE HELPED SCREW YOU OVER

"Resentment is like drinking poison and then hoping it will kill your enemies."

– Nelson Mandela

One day I was talking with a friend, he told me several people had screwed him over and it's basically ruined his life. What he was saying was 100% true. There were people in his life that have royally fucked him over. However, to convince yourself that your life is ruined because of a few incidents is madness. You can always pick yourself back up and succeed in life!

Many of us will encounter being screwed over in our lives. If you never encounter this from somebody that you trust, then consider yourself one of the lucky ones. It's not a pleasant experience, but it's something that we can all move on from.

Have you ever invested lots of time, effort, or money into a relationship where you genuinely wanted to do your best for someone?

You have helped that person enormously and they no longer give a shit about you. As far as they're concerned, it's all about them, and when you need their help, they turn their back and don't help you in your time of need.

After helping someone, they don't help you in return. Maybe they stop showing an interest in you, and they don't pick up your calls as readily as they once did when they needed you.

If you've been through this type of situation, I know exactly how you feel because it's happened to me. But it hasn't just happened to us, it's happened to millions of people around the world.

When someone screws you over, it's like being on a military assault course and you've both come to a wall. You've helped push them over the wall when they were struggling to get over it. Of course, you'd expect them to help you and pull you up. However, rather than them staying on top of the wall and pulling you up, they've just fucked off and run off into the sunset!

When this type of thing happens to us, we have two choices at this point. We can think about how life is not fair and how someone or some circumstance in life has screwed us over; or we can put our big boy pants on, move forward, and create a glorious life for ourselves.

When we replay in our mind some injustice and we feel

resentment towards someone, we only hurt ourselves and cause our own unhappiness. It would be extremely easy for me to feel some resentment towards Sergeant Goddard, but what good would that do? I sincerely hope he found happiness and would wish him all the best in life. If I saw him now, I'd probably say hi and ask him what he's been doing since his army days. I probably wouldn't spend an evening watching the sun go down with him or have a candle lit dinner with him, but I don't hate him. Even though I have every reason to do so.

I probably wouldn't even go out for a coffee with him, but the reason for that is mainly because of how much I value my time. I usually only ever go out for a coffee or lunch with family and friends.

Like yourself, I've been initially shocked at the behaviour of some people when I helped them get what they want, and they didn't come to my aid when I asked them for help. Some people I've helped in the past now ignore me, because they got what they needed out of me and are now looking for new opportunities. Have you had this happen to you? If you've been on this planet for long enough, you probably have.

I had a best friend that moved away to Southampton, England. It was one of those relationships where you could go for months without seeing somebody, and then, when you see them again, you talk just like you have seen them a day or two ago. We were close friends for the best part of 30 years.

After several months of not hearing from him, one day I had a phone call from him out of the blue. He was struggling financially, and he asked me if I could lend him money to pay his mortgage that month. I said yes, no problem and transferred the money over to his account. Around a week later, I WhatsApp'd him, and asked him how he was. I could see from the blue double tick he had read my message, but he didn't reply.

During that week, I phoned him twice, but he didn't answer his phone. I messaged him again a couple of times to ask if he was okay and saw that he'd received and read my messages. Still, he didn't reply. I didn't care about the money and messaged him to say that he could keep the money as a gift, and I didn't want it back.

As several weeks went by, I tried to phone him again, but he didn't respond. And that was the end of our 30-year relationship.

Thank you for your money and goodbye!

Ironically, I didn't even need his help for anything. In fact,

I would've probably helped him out a little more financially if he asked.

As I write these words, I had a little chuckle to myself about the situation, but at the time I thought it was a shame that our friendship ended that way. One minute you are the best thing since sliced bread to someone, and the next minute they won't give you the time of day.

Maybe you've helped someone before, and they no longer want anything to do with you. As strange as that may seem, it just happens sometimes in life. I remember having a conversation with my mum about how strange some people are, and she said,

"You've just got to accept people for who they are."

She was right!

I've been really pissed off with certain people because of how selfish they were. I kept on replaying the words in my head such as,

"Why won't they help me when I've changed their life for the better?"

"This is crazy. This isn't fair, this isn't something that I would do, this is morally wrong!"

"What was the point in me helping them so much?"

"Have I just wasted my time with them?"

"I'm a nice person and I help people. Why aren't I rewarded as much as certain people that are horrible and don't give a fuck about anyone apart from themselves?"

This list can go on and on. Oh yes, I've said all of these things to myself throughout my life. I threw myself several pity-parties over the last 47 years because of one injustice or another.

You probably have a few examples like this from your own life?

In the end, I realised that all of this negative energy that I was feeling towards someone was just hurting me.

I remember going on a date with a girl and she was talking about her ex-husband. She told me that her son was nine years old and her ex-husbands other son, from the woman he is now with, is eight and a half years old. When she told me this, there was a moment of silence. It was as if she could hear the cogs turning in my head. I looked at her and said,

"Soooooooooo."

Before I could say anything else, she said, "Yes he was having an affair."

It must've hurt at the time, but rather than ask her about that, I asked her how she feels about the whole thing now. She told me she is fine about it all and said his new wife is a lovely person.

I told her that's the best way to think about it.

Your happiness depends on how you interpret the situation!

You never really know what somebody is genuinely thinking. For all I know, she could still be pissed about the affair. Many would! However, if she has truly let it go and has moved on with her life, she has done the right thing for herself and her child.

When someone takes advantage of you and screws you over, you can either resent them and hold bitter feelings within yourself, or you can stay strong, let that resentment go, and find happiness.

So, when someone screws you over, or they no longer want anything to do with you, just understand it's part of life's little game.

This may not be what you want to hear, but for your own sake and your own mental health, you must now toughen up and move forward with your life!

CHAPTER 5

DO IT YOURSELF

"It takes half your life before you discover life is a do-it-yourself project."
– Napoleon Hill

As I mentioned in the previous two chapters, it's easy to think about people who screwed us over and blame them for a whole variety of things. And it's easy to get upset with people that you've helped, but they've turned their back on you when you've needed them most.

Some people are takers and that's just the way they are. They're focused on themselves and give little thought to others. However, when they don't help people who have been there for them, they shoot themselves in the foot.

When the givers in life stop helping selfish people, the selfish people then complain that others should help them more. That's how they are, and the chances are, there's nothing that you or I can do about it.

When you've gone the extra mile for someone and when you need them, but they won't give you the time of day, it's easy to feel deflated and hard done by.

However, you must let them go and not dwell on their lack of support for you. If you keep thinking about how much you've done for them, and how they don't give a shit about you anymore, negative thoughts can fester in your mind. The problem with holding onto resentment is it will hamper your ability to achieve your own goals and can prevent you living a happy and fulfilled life.

Rather than get upset about what's happened, use the situation to motivate you. You must take action and do things yourself.

With or without them, you are a champion!

Your success and happiness doesn't depend on certain individuals.

Some people who you've helped don't want you to succeed. They could be friends, family, or members of the public. This can be a harsh pill to swallow because friends and family should help you and should want you to win in life. However, some of them will feel threatened if you achieve more than them. They want you to succeed, but not succeed more than them. They want you to climb up to a certain rung of the ladder, but not past them. Some of them will sneakily even make moves to keep you back in life.

I have a friend who I knew from school. In school my friend was one of 'The Main Men.' He was cool, he was good looking, he was slim, he was good with the girls and he had a no fucks given attitude. However, wind the clock forward 25 years, he had now grown a big belly and felt depressed when I spoke to him.

Fortunately, my friend has now lost all of his weight, and when I spoke to him, it was like talking to a different person. It was great to see how much his life had transformed. However, he told me that several of his friends were telling him he had lost too much weight.

The reality of the situation was, he hadn't. He was eating nutritious food five or six times a day and was training six days a week. I reassured him he didn't look too skinny and told him that his friends were probably jealous. They were used to seeing the overweight version of him and didn't like who he had become because he was now in better shape than most of his friends. His friends wanted to pull him back to where he once was, so they could feel better about their own lack of achievement.

My friend didn't have a personal fitness trainer to help him six days a week, so he went out there and did it all himself. He eats well and consistently does physical exercise, and it paid off for him, big-time!

I watched a few TV Military programs and how some of the ex-soldiers talk about how everybody in the forces is a team and you always go the extra mile for one another. Some people in the military will go the extra mile for their friends. They'll even go the extra mile for people they don't know. But to believe that every single person in the military is somebody who will put others in front of themselves is a facade to say the least.

Do you think Sergeant Goddard would have put his life on the line for me in a conflict? That question made me chuckle while I'm writing these words. You may know or have known people who are more likely to put a bullet in your back, than do the whole Kevin Costner Bodyguard scene, where he takes a bullet for his boss. Oh yes, and she was his lover. Thankfully, Sergeant Goddard was just my boss and had no romantic feelings towards me.

In the British military there is a system called the 'buddy-buddy system' where you help your fellow soldier. This can be helping each other put on heavy bergens (backpacks) or pushing others to get over a wall.

However, behind-the-scenes all is not what it seems. Military people are still people. Some are awesome, and some are, well, not so awesome. This is true of any profession in life, and there will be times where you simply can't rely on others and you have to do things yourself!

I have succeeded with many things in life when others have doubted me or turned their back on me, and I have done this by telling myself I can succeed.

To think that all of your hopes and dreams rely on one or two individuals is foolish. Yes, we all need others to help us on our journey with life. However, sometimes the people who you thought would be there for you, won't be there, and others who you thought wouldn't help you helped you achieve your goals.

I know it's a positive mental attitude cliché, but to succeed in this life, you must have that 'I CAN' attitude!

Some people have more of an 'I CAN' attitude than others. It can be the way they are naturally. Some people naturally have an 'I CAN'T' attitude. Do you know anybody like this?

Maybe you're like me. I have an 'I can' attitude but I also need to read, listen, and watch positive material to help me achieve my goals. I often get this positive mental attitude by reading personal development books, listening to music, and watching an inspirational documentary.

I know an author who was rejected over 100 times by publishing companies and agents, but kept telling himself that he could be successful. To help him on his way, he wrote his goals and who he wanted to be on a set of cards, which he called goal cards. After he had written what he wanted out of life on these goal cards, he read the cards every day to enforce it in his mind that he would achieve these things.

On one of these goal cards, he wrote he was a six-figure income a year author. As the years went by, he still didn't have any success, but he kept on reading those cards to himself. He never stopped believing that one day he could become a success, despite many people thinking his goals were unrealistic.

He not only achieved his goal of becoming a six-figure income author and earning $100,000 a year, but he also now earns over $1 million a year. The six-figure income dream turned out to be a seven-figure income!

When he was rejected by these experts in the publishing industry, he had every reason to give up, but he never did. He ploughed forward, became a self-published author without traditional publishing deals and made things happen himself!

So, when your friends, family, colleagues, or the so-called experts won't help you achieve your goals… do it yourself!

CHAPTER 6

LAZY WITH LUXURY

"It's tough to get out of bed to do roadwork at 5am when you've been sleeping in silk pyjamas."
– Marvellous Marvin Hagler

Not getting the help and support off people who should help you is one thing, but many people become lazy because of the luxurious life we now live compared to people hundreds of years ago

Today, we have so many things done for us, we can, often without realising it, become lazy and mentally weak.

People have never had it so good. There has never been a time throughout history where so many innovators have invented products or created services that make life a lot easier for us. Naturally, we use these inventions and services to our advantage.

However, because we are used to having things done for us, it can make us mentally weak and lazy. When we think that someone, some company, or some government should do things for us, we are wasting valuable time and can fall into victim mode mentality. Both of these things put the brakes on living life to the full!

Here is a classic example of wasting time because we wait for people to do something that we could do ourselves.

One morning, I dropped my son Léon off to school and then hit the gym. After the gym, I went shopping at Tesco's. As I was heading towards the checkout, I noticed there were big lines of people waiting to use the aisles where the checkout girls were. Nothing that we all haven't seen in a supermarket before. But what amused me was, many of the people waiting to be served at the checkout only had a small amount of shopping.

As for me, I headed to the express checkout, scanned my shopping, and left. When I left, there were still people who queued up before me, still waiting to see the checkout girls.

There are two main reasons they didn't want to use the express checkout. These are because they:

1. Have a habit of using a checkout where somebody serves them.

2. Are too lazy to scan the items themselves.

There is also a third reason which is people become like sheep and just like to join queues. That may be because they feel safe amongst other people. Some people who struggle with anxiety or are or a bag of nerves can find going to the express checkout a scary thing. This may seem ludicrous to some people, but we have to take people from where they are. However, the vast majority of people have more confidence than that.

They could've gone straight to the express checkout and used either cash or a card to pay for the items they were purchasing. However, they didn't want to think about scanning the items themselves. They wanted someone to do it for them, even though they wasted valuable time by queuing longer.

That's how lazy many people have now become in society. They stand there like a bunch of zombies waiting in line, when they could scan the items themselves. If they did that, they could use the time they had wasted to do something more productive with their day.

They are the type of people that don't exercise, eat lots of saturated fat and sugary foods, and wait for a scientist to invent a pill that can make them lose weight.

"Oh shit, did I just pigeon-hole some people? Yeah, my bad."

Some of them buy a lottery ticket and put their hopes and dreams on luck rather than improving themselves so they can become more valuable to others and get paid more. It's not that there's anything wrong with buying a lottery ticket. Some of the money goes to noble causes. However, if your hopes and your dreams are pinned on the luck of the lottery, there's a good chance you're going to be disappointed throughout your entire life.

Some people enjoy going to the supermarket and buying necessities for their house. However, if you're more like me, going to the supermarket is just something that needs to be done. But why not use that time to do something productive?

I often have my headphones plugged into one of my ears and listen to an audiobook on personal development. This way, I'm learning something with this otherwise wasted time. Or I listen to music to lift my spirits while shopping. Of course, another option these days, is to pay somebody to do your shopping for you or use a home shopping delivery service.

Time is the most precious commodity we have, so it's vital that we use it wisely. To live the best quality and the most productive life we can, we need to think about where we are spending our time every day and we also need to do things ourselves.

No one can do your press ups for you; you have to put the

effort in to get the results you want!

Sometimes you'll need to wait for other people who specialise in a certain field to help you achieve your goals. However, if you can do something efficiently, then put the effort into getting it done. It can often be much quicker to do things yourself rather than waiting around for other people all day long!

CHAPTER 7

RISE ABOVE YOUR BACKGROUND

"It doesn't matter where you're from. You can be from the hood or the suburbs. You can be poor with no education or college graduate. No matter your background, you can win."

– Lil B

On 4th December 1969, a baby called Shawn was born in Brooklyn, New York.

When he was a boy, Shawn loved listening to Michael Jackson and used to dance around to his music.

He always wanted to be the best at anything he did, such as basketball, and when he would lose the game, he would challenge his friends to another game.

He was a very bright kid according to his family and was in some of the top classes in school although he never graduated, and he used to stay out late tapping on the table and practising his rap songs.

He listened again and again to rap songs and even looked in the dictionary for inspiration, because he wanted to find words that would rhyme with the words he had thought of.

When he was younger there was a big crack cocaine epidemic where he lived in Marcy Projects, and it wasn't exactly what you would call a peaceful, friendly neighbourhood!

Where I grew up, the most likely thing that you would get shot with was an air rifle by one of your (so-called) friends or in my case by my older brother.

In Shawn's area, they were using Uzi submachine guns!

In the tough projects of Brooklyn, one minute children could be out playing Double Dutch waiting for the ice-cream van to come along and the next minute there would be bullets flying all over the place! When the coast was clear and the gunmen had gone, the children would come back out to play; that was the way of life in his neighbourhood.

When he was only nine-years old, Shawn saw somebody get shot dead in the hallway of his apartment building, which as you can imagine had a big effect on him!

He looked up to his dad more than anybody else in the world and classed dad as a superhero, but when Shawn was roughly 12-years old, his father moved out, which broke his heart; it was a very traumatic time in young Shawn's life!

However, his mother was a strong woman; she inspired him and told him he could be anything he wanted to be!

Shawn's mother told him that "What you put into something is what you get out of something," which he took to heart.

His mum bought him his first boombox stereo and his mum's friend bought him his first paper notepad so he could write lyrics.

Shawn enjoyed sitting at the table writing lyrics for hours on end and never believed that anything would come out of it, because he didn't feel it was hard work. It was simply something that he loved to do.

Although Shawn loved going out with his friends and playing basketball, he had found a new love in writing songs and performing them, even if it was only to himself in his bedroom.

So, most of his time was spent working on his new love, writing, and rapping.

However, perhaps without a strong father figure being there to guide him, he was influenced by drug dealers and became a drug dealer himself, selling things like crack cocaine. Shawn knew he could make lots of money from it and in his area, it was just a way of life.

He was fed up with being where he was, and he wanted to become a big player in life, but he was more interested in being a big player in the music industry rather than a drug dealer.

Shawn started hanging around his friend Jazz, who was also into music.

Shawn was later featured in Jazz's rap video, but it didn't take off in the big way that he hoped it would.

He then hooked up with another friend and they went to play gigs together.

When Shawn was first introduced on stage, he didn't get the warmest of welcomes but when he started rapping things changed!

Unfortunately, he still didn't get the breakthrough that he wanted, so he went back to the street and started selling crack again.

However, he had a friend who believed in him and his friend persuaded him to go back to rapping.

As much as Shawn tried to make it in the business he

faced rejection, after rejection, after rejection from music industry labels and sometimes he doubted whether he was going to get signed to a record label, but this was his ultimate dream so he persisted and he kept going!

Shawn decided that there were too many gatekeepers in the way to his success so, instead of asking a record label to produce his songs, he created his own record label and went public doing his own gigs.

Shawn's audience was growing, and he was seeing more success, but there were also disappointments ahead when the venues he had booked got poor ticket sales. At one point his ticket sales for his tour were so bad Shawn and his team quit the tour halfway through.

At the same time he quit the tour, one of Shawn's team heard the beat to the song 'It's A Hard Knock Life' (from the musical 'Annie') and bought the rights so Shawn could release it as a track.

It was a massive success, and Shawn's life changed forever; he later picked up a Grammy Award for this track and became more widely known through his stage name… JAY-Z.

After that happened, JAY-Z and his team went on tour and sold out almost every show!

He also collaborated with other hip-hop artists, which opened many doors for them as well.

JAY-Z said he still believes what you put out in the world, you get back and how you treat people is how you get treated!

Even though he grew up in a dangerous area, he believes that was a good thing because it taught him how to survive and he turned many negative situations into positive events in his head.

He was always incredibly grateful to his mother and said that he had a brilliant upbringing.

Although there are many people out there whose parents aren't as supportive as his mum, that doesn't mean you can't be successful as there are countless people out there that have made a success of their lives and whose parents haven't supported them wholeheartedly in their endeavours.

His main goal when he is putting out music is to tell the truth and to connect to people on a deeper level, so it can help them with their own lives.

Although he has 'made it' in the world, he still believes he is a student of music and there is always more to learn and that he has learned far more from failures than he has from success.

He drew on inspirational figures such as Martin Luther King Junior and Michael Jordan and has said that he borrows certain character traits such as strength, courage, and determination from inspirational people.

He believes that belief in yourself is what makes all the difference to whether you fail or succeed.

One thing that JAY-Z did towards being successful was he was constantly putting records out; the more records he put out, the more opportunities would come his way!

If you just put one or two records out, or if you're an author and you just put 1, 2, 3 or 4 books out in your life, there is no way you can guarantee much success.

However, when you put out 10, 20, 30, or 40 different products, it is almost certain to make a difference!

The higher your work rate is, the more likely you are to succeed!

Even when he became more successful, he would still have little failures and he would have his critics waiting to come out and criticise him, but he kept going!

When he was interviewed on the Swedish chat show Skavlan, the interviewer said, "You're comparing yourself to Frank Sinatra, a Scandinavian wouldn't have the nerve to do it, but you have?"

JAY-Z said, "It's always good to compare yourself to people you look up to because you give yourself a high goal, you set high standards for yourself. How he affected the culture is what I strive to do, (so I) set the bar really high!"

In 2006, MTV ranked him as the greatest MC of all time.

At the time of writing, according to Wikipedia, JAY-Z has sold over 100-million records and received 21 Grammy Awards. In 2020, Forbes estimated his net worth at $1 billion.

He's also a very generous person with giving to charities.

At the current time of writing this book, JAY-Z, CEO of Twitter – Jack Dorsey and Rhianna all teamed up to give more than $6 million to the COVID-19 relief effort.

JAY-Z became an inspiration for not only people from the ghetto but for people all over the world!

Let's look at back on JAY-Z's life and see what factors led

him to become such an incredible success.

- It doesn't matter what your circumstances are when you're younger, you can be successful.

- It doesn't matter what neighbourhood you grow up in, you can be successful.

- It doesn't matter if you don't have the perfect family life, you can be successful.

- Follow your heart and do what you love to do.

- Put a lot of time and effort into what you love.

- Keep going even when you get lots of rejection.

- Get around friends and family that believe in you.

- If the establishment is always rejecting you, set up your own establishment, no matter how small at first.

- What you put out into the world is what you get back.

- Treat people like you'd like to be treated yourself.

- Be grateful to the people who have helped you along the way.
- Connect with people on a deep level.
- Collaborate with other people so it opens more doors for you.
- Learn from your failures.
- There is always more to learn, no matter how successful you are.
- Turn negative situations into positive situations.
- Learn off other people.
- Put out lots of products consistently.
- Keep going regardless of what your critics say.
- Learn about inspirational people and draw power from what you have learnt.
- Believe in yourself.

CHAPTER 8

CELEBRATE SMALL VICTORIES

"Take your victories whatever they may be."
– Mia Hamm

One of my friends has been going through a hard time in her life. She could no longer cope with facing work, so she took some time off to get her head together. Unfortunately, taking a couple of weeks off led to a couple of months off and she has now been off work for many years.

When I saw her, she said that she doesn't enjoy going out of the house anymore because it frightens her.

I could see she was very fragile and the last thing she needed to hear is somebody say man the fuck up and sort your shit out. Some people are strong enough to take that sort of advice, and others crumble far easier.

My friend needed a bit more empathy, and I told her she just needs to take things one step at a time. She told me that her family would be better off if she weren't in this world.

Sometimes people get so overwhelmed with life, they feel

they can no longer cope and think they and others that know them would be better off if they weren't in this world. If you've read my book, 'Man The F*ck Up,' you'll already know that my mum, my grandad, and my dad's cousin all killed themselves. In that book I forgot to mention that my great uncle also killed himself, so my family has quite the track record.

When she told me, she believed others would be better off if she wasn't in this world. Any sympathy I gave her got tossed out of the window. This is where I go from my compassionate side to giving them a harsh dose of reality. I tell them in no uncertain terms how much pain and suffering they would cause the rest of their family. I have had several friends that have been mollycoddled too much by others and they ended up killing themselves.

When people get to a state of depression sometimes, it's very hard to focus on anybody else apart from themselves. I know this because I've been there myself.

I also told her she needed to take one step at a time, and she should try to achieve small goals that meant something to her. Achieving small goals would help lift her out of her depression, because they would give her more self-worth.

You don't have to run a successful business, earn a shit

load of money, break records, or anything else to feel you are winning. You just need to take one step at a time and achieve things bit by bit.

A few days after I spoke to my friend, I got a text message from her. She said that she'd spoken to someone she hardly knew, and she felt like it was a victory. This was when I knew my little pep-talk had worked.

My friend told me it might sound stupid to think just talking to a person she never met before was a victory. However, I knew it was far from stupid and I told her so. She felt it was a personal victory, and I confirmed to her it was a significant achievement and a step in the right direction.

When you achieve something that is significant to you, it's a victory! No matter how small you think others may think your victory is, it is a victory to you, and that's all that matters!

If someone belittles your victory, you don't need that person in your life. However, if that person is still in your life, then it's best to keep your thoughts to yourself and only tell your victories to the friends that support you. But sometimes, you don't need to tell anybody about your victories. These are the quiet victories that don't need to go any further than your own mind.

You never need somebody else to validate you, it's up to you to validate yourself!

Editing the final chapters of this book was a victory to me. To some writers, editing several chapters of a book is child's play, and they think little of it.

While I was writing the last parts of this chapter, it was a Sunday. The sun was shining, and people were walking around and enjoying their time off work. I knew there were more leisurely things I could do, but I also knew my deadline for publishing this book was only a handful of days away and I had to get it done. There would be other days when I could take time off, but this wasn't one of them.

It's always the hardest at the start. When I woke up on this day, I knew I had to work for around 10 or 12 hours. To do this, I had to get myself in the right frame of mind. As soon as I woke up, I picked up my iPad and started editing. I wanted to start strongly. I went into it with the same mindset as when I did a 50-mile run in the Sahara Desert. At the start of that run I thought to myself, I'm just going to run all day, and anything else is a bonus.

As the minutes and hours rolled by with my editing, the more I enjoyed it. I got to the stage where I didn't want to stop writing and editing. No matter how nice the weather was outside and no matter what leisure activities I could be doing, I just wanted to edit and write.

Maybe you've experienced this yourself? It might have been when you did an exercise. Getting out of the door and starting the exercise was difficult, but when you were five or ten minutes into the exercise, it became easier and more enjoyable. When you enjoy what you are doing, things flow much easier and as time goes on, you have scored some points for yourself.

When you are enjoying something, you also lose your sense of time. Think back to a time when you've been enjoying yourself and time just flew by. You can probably think back to times when something is boring and you're counting the seconds for the activity to finish. For example, one hour down the beach on a warm summer's day would fly by a lot quicker than half an hour in the dentist's chair.

In the end I ended up working for 13 1/2 hours, I had almost completed the book and felt a great sense of accomplishment.

When we accomplish what we set out to accomplish, it makes us feel incredibly good about ourselves. But if you can feel good about yourself while you are doing your exercise, project, business, or whatever else it is you are working on, then that's a double win!

When my friend started talking to somebody, she felt nervous at first and wanted the conversation to end. However, as the conversation went on, she thought about how well she was doing, which encouraged her to keep on talking. When she had finished the conversation, she knew she had accomplished something great!

By facing what she feared and taking action, it had a lasting positive impact on her for the rest of her day. Sadly, my friend's fear often puts the brakes on her life, and she misses out on lots of wonderful experiences.

The last thing anybody who is in a delicate frame of mind needs to hear is something like, "Why don't you run a marathon, that's more of a victory."

This would be very detrimental to her, as she just wasn't at that level. The most important step for her was to get out of her house and overcome her fear of going outside.

On the other side of the coin, you could win all the awards and get all the money in the world, but if you don't feel you're succeeding, it doesn't matter.

No matter what stage you are in your life, the more you run yourself down by not celebrating your small victories, the more negative you will become in life.

The person who can walk 1 mile and feel good about what they have achieved will feel better than someone who runs 30 miles and feels disappointed. That might sound ridiculous to some people, but you'd be surprised how many people run themselves down even when they're achieving great things. I know people that earn several hundred thousand pounds a year, but are disappointed because they feel it's not enough. They often compare themselves with somebody else that is making more money, and this makes them feel sad.

Beating yourself up by comparing your successes with others is foolish! If you want to feel better about yourself and live a happy and healthier life, simply concentrate on your own goals, and celebrate your own victories, no matter how large or small they may be.

If you are in a situation and you want to improve things, then you have to change what you are doing by being bold and taking massive action!

You should never apologise for where you are in life. You are where you are in life, and if someone else has got a problem with it, that's their problem, not yours.

So just to summarise, you should never belittle your own

victories. No matter what anyone else thinks, they are your victories, so treasure them. By treasuring your own successes in life, you will build your self-confidence and you will achieve greater things. You deserve the best things in life, so go out there and claim them!

CHAPTER 9

ARE YOU OK DOWN THERE?

"No act of kindness, no matter how small, is ever wasted."
– Aesop

The rain poured down in my hometown of Haverfordwest and I was getting squashed by the crowd. I was seven years old. The year was 1981.

I was a little boy amongst a sea of adults when Lady Diana leaned forward and said to me, "Are you ok down there?"

I'd never spoken to someone who was part of the royal family, or should I say, who was about to become a part of the royal family. I didn't quite know how to reply. I didn't know whether I should look her in the eye, but she seemed to have a warm, kind-hearted way about her.

Thousands of people were lined up in the streets just to see her and Prince Charles. To say I was surprised she asked little ol me how I felt was a shock. All I knew was this was a huge occasion for our little town, and I felt I had to be overly polite to her.

"Yes, thank you very much Mam," I shyly and awkwardly replied.

I thought I'd messed up what I had said to her, but she warmly smiled and walked off.

I remember thinking to myself,

"Out of all the far more important adults here wanting your attention, why would you stop and talk to me? Even more strangely, why would you care about me? I'm just an insignificant small boy compared to the surrounding grownups."

16 years later I was finishing a guard shift in 29 Commando's main base, the Royal Citadel in Plymouth.

I pointed my rifle at the sandbank to do my unloading drill, and when I had finished, I walked towards the guardroom. On my way to the guardroom, the soldier outside told me Princess Diana had been killed in a car crash in Paris.

There are only two times in my life where I can remember where I was when something big happened in the news. One was when The Twin Towers fell in New York, and the other was when Princess Diana died. You've probably had similar experiences yourself where you can remember what you were doing and where you were when something big and tragic happened.

Princess Diana did a lot of incredible things in her life, but what I remember most about her was when she asked me how I was.

She showed compassion even when she didn't need to. I

was a stranger to her, but it was kind and it made a difference to a little boy. When she spoke to me, I wasn't desperately in need of help. However, I thought it was nice that she cared, and she seemed very genuine.

I later learned in life, it doesn't matter whether a princess or a pauper shows compassion. What matters is that some people show compassion when you are hurting the most.

There will be times in our lives when we go through heartache and where others show compassion towards us. This can make a difference to you, and you can take comfort in knowing that somebody cares about what you are going through. You may have already experienced this in your own life.

There is always someone that needs help. Chances are, some of your friends and family will need your help and compassion at some point. But it's not just friends and relatives we should show compassion to, it could be anyone.

Considering the title of this book and many of my other books, it would be easy for a reader to think that I am just a cold-hearted bastard that tells you to put your big boy pants on and man the fuck up. Sometimes people don't respond to compassion and they need a kick up the arse. However, when they have just gone through a traumatic situation, this is obviously not the time.

There are always pros and cons to social media. However, one positive with social media is we can see we are not alone in the tough times. Hardships come to everyone, no matter who you are or how lucky you are.

I go through periods where I don't read the newsfeeds but when I do, it seems there are people who are going through heart-breaking challenges. And even in the weeks where I don't see this, you can guarantee that someone is suffering. Maybe you didn't see their post on your newsfeed, or maybe they are keeping their challenges to themselves.

The day before I wrote these words, I read a Facebook post from a friend I used to hang around with when we had our little 50cc motorbikes at 16. He posted that his mum had just died. After seeing this post, I messaged my friend and his dad to say my thoughts are with them at this challenging time.

Within that same week, I had been corresponding with a friend who had been in the special forces and suffers with post-traumatic stress disorder (PTSD).

That same week I met up with my friend Efrem Brynin, who travelled down from Sussex to go to an event at a military camp called Brawdy, which is close to where I live. His son James was based in Brawdy with 16 Signal Regiment and was tragically killed in Afghanistan when he was only 22. To make things even worse, he was killed by a soldier on the same side as him.

Before I saw Efrem that morning, I posted about me receiving the first copy of 'Put Your Big Boy Pants On.' I could see that one of the first people that loved the post is a friend whose 15-year-old daughter took her own life several years before.

Within days of these things happening, my friend and former Royal Marine Commando Gordon Smith posted these words:

"Today I have the rest of my life. Over the last few days, I have had the news that the cancer I had is back and terminal with a short end of life.

Obviously my family and close friends are all aware, I now wish to extend this news to friends on Facebook. I have had wonderful support from people all over, with some wishes of support from customers 20 years ago.

Thank you for the support and love.

I now enter end-of-life plans and hopefully go home to journey on... I will endeavour to keep you up to date. I am well, spirit is strong, no regret (well maybe a couple)."

Journey well, Gordon xx

Within the same month, an old school friend of mine announced that his 21-year-old daughter has been killed in a car crash.

Life can be amazing, and life can be brutal. We don't make the rules, it's just the way it is. And if we had a choice, we'd all want to miss out on the brutal things that happen in our lives. Sadly, this is impossible.

There is a time and a place for telling people to toughen up, and there is a time and a place for showing compassion. Of course, you don't need the brains of a rocket scientist to know when somebody has just gone through a traumatic time, this is a time when compassion needs to be shown. It is also the time when people need compassion the most.

However, sometimes in life it's easy to think about our own challenges and forget about how tough things are for other people. Of course, we don't need to only show compassion to people when one of their loved ones dies. Compassion can be given in many circumstances when people are struggling.

A few years ago when my financial situation was bad, I was having a little sulk and was thinking to myself, 'How am I going to pay my bills and take my son to nice places when I haven't got a job and have no money?'

Things were grim, and I was struggling to stay positive, so I went to the gym to lift my spirits. I did an hour of running, which was more than I had done for a while, and then did 80 minutes on the exercise bike. Training on the treadmill and the exercise bike had lifted my spirits, but I still didn't feel 100%, and still wasn't in a positive state of mind.

After my training I hit the sauna, where I met a guy who was overweight and is the same age as me. He told me he had lost a lot of weight and wanted to lose more.

I knew I wasn't where I wanted to be in life, but I also knew the guy I was talking to also wasn't. His major challenge was his obesity.

Rather than tell him about the current things that weren't perfect in my life, I turned my focus to helping him. I told him how I was overweight once and told him about some of my physical achievements. I never told him about my achievements to say, "Hey look at me aren't I great." I told him about them to say, "If I can do these things, then you can lose four stone and turn your life around."

After telling him about where I had come from, I could see hope in his eyes.

Within a brief space of time, by going to the gym, I had achieved several things. I had:

- Helped my mental frame of mind by going out and doing some fitness training.

- Lifted someone's spirits and had given them hope.

I also felt better about myself because I helped him.

Some people don't like helping others. They dwell on their own problems and they feel they shouldn't help others when they have their own challenges to sort out. Some people don't like helping others because they don't want others to succeed. They would rather see them fail because they can feel they have one up on them. And after all, why should someone else feel happy when they're not.

Thinking like that is a sad way to live your life, and it helps no one. That sort of thinking is not only detrimental to the other person's mental health because you haven't helped them; but it is also detrimental to your own mental health when you think negatively towards somebody else.

It's amazing the satisfaction you get from helping people

and showing compassion when someone is down. It gives you an inner wealth that money can't buy. And the more you help others, the more likely the universe will help you in return. It may not be from the person you helped, but it will come back to you.

CHAPTER 10

STRUGGLE SELF-TALK AND SUCCESS

"Dream, struggle, create, prevail.
Be daring. Be brave. Be strong. Be brilliant."
– Katrina Fake

We all have inner conversations with ourselves, but what most people don't realise is positive inner conversation or negative inner conversation is a habit.

After the release of my book, 'Man The F*ck Up,' I had to rearrange speaking events because of the COVID-19 situation. I kept on working on the writing and publishing, but, as with this book, I initially struggled with the editing because I was thrown off track by my other business.

Once you break a habit, it can be harder to get back into that habit. Because there are so many aspects involved with writing and publishing books, I sometimes find it challenging doing lots of different activities.

I find it easier in my little comfort zone doing one type of work every day, but that's not the way things work in the publishing world, and indeed sometimes in life.

Sometimes I would open up my Word document to edit

my forthcoming books, and after a few minutes I would shut off the Word document because I wanted to do something else. I'd rather go for a spin in my boat or kick back and watch a movie, because they're both effortless.

I had written hundreds of thousands of words that needed editing and juggling all these words with everything else that was going on in my life was a challenge.

Many people's dreams die with them because they never acted on achieving their goals. That's not what you want out of life, and neither do I.

You can live one of two lives.

One life is the life where you take risks and take massive action towards your goals and you persist until you succeed. And the other life is where you don't take risks, put little effort in, and give up on your dreams too easily.

I don't know about you, but in years to come I want to look back at my life and know that I didn't sell myself short by making excuses, being lazy and giving up too easily.

Whenever I struggle with certain aspects of writing and publishing, I tell myself the reasons why I need to put the work in and get more books out.

Some reasons are because:

1. It will provide a better income for myself and my son and give us the freedom to do more things in life.

2. It will help lots of people achieve their own goals and dreams.

3. Every book I write and publish is something I can look back on and be proud of.

What are your reasons for taking actions towards your goals?

The more powerful the reason you have to put the work in, the more likely you are to do the things that need to be done.

I started telling myself that it was easy to edit my books and also told myself the reasons why I needed to produce books and the process became easier. Nothing changed except my thoughts about what I was doing.

When you change your thinking, you can change your life!

Initially, I was telling myself editing was hard, and I'd rather be doing something else. The problem with this negative self-talk is, it gets wired into your brain the more you repeat it. Whether or not something is true, you make it true in your own mind by repeating the words again and again. We all have negative self-talk, especially when something goes wrong in our lives. But rather than beat ourselves up, we must intervene and feed our minds with positive self-talk.

There hasn't been one aspect of publishing and writing that I haven't struggled to do at one point or another. They have been several times where I didn't want to:

- Do research.
- Write.
- Edit.
- Send messages that needed to be sent.
- Learn about different marketing strategies
- Implement different marketing strategies.
- Ask people for reviews.
- And an entire load of other things involved in the publishing world.

I knew I needed to cut out my negative self-talk and replace it with positive self-talk. Also, when you repeat your negative self-talk in one area of your life, it can affect other areas of your life negatively, just as positive self-talk will.

When a child is learning to walk, it often falls down, but it keeps trying until it walks. The child doesn't try to walk for one or two days and give up, it tries until it succeeds. We must do the same thing. We must keep going no matter how many times we have failed.

When you're faced with a challenge, you must:

- Think about your plan of action.
- Attack the problem.
- And keep going until things get easier.

When you need to get certain things done, it can be uncomfortable. Chances are you're going to have to roll your sleeves up, put in the work, and make things happen. This requires a particular mindset. It may not always be the easiest thing to do, and yes it can be really tough. However, it's necessary to make lots of progress and achieve your goals!

To get a genuine sense of fulfilment in life and grow our self-worth, we must tackle hard challenges!

It's the same with fitness training, you've got to get out of the door and put the effort in. And the more you make these things a habit, and tell yourself that they are easy, the easier the activities become!

So, flood your mind with that 'I CAN' attitude, and take massive action towards your goals!

CHAPTER 11

CAN CHANGE, CAN'T CHANGE, SHOULDN'T CHANGE

"Guilt is a cancer. Guilt will confine you, torture you and destroy you."
– Dave Grohl

One day my friend sent me a message on WhatsApp. The message showed a picture of Hong Kong in 1964 and compared it to Hong Kong in 2021.

Because I know my friend so well, I knew what he was thinking. The earlier photo in 1964 showed how Hong Kong was a much greener and natural place than the skyscraper packed Hong Kong in 2021. I knew my friend would be thinking about how humans as a species are ruining the planet by erecting skyscrapers along with other buildings where people work.

My friend gets very depressed about these things. I can see where he's coming from. I love seeing a place of natural beauty that industry has not touched, and we are lucky to still have many of those places all over the world.

However, getting upset about the evolution of the human race is counter-productive to living a happy life.

My friend often focuses on the negative side of things, so I messaged him back and told him I knew exactly what he was thinking. However, without buildings and technology racing forward like it is, the world would be a much worse place. My friend never stopped to think about how his family benefits from industry. And many of the luxuries that my friend and his family use today have come from people working in buildings.

For example, the car he drives, the TV he watches, the computer he uses and just about everything in his house has come from people producing products and services in buildings. And yes, as harsh as it may seem to some, trees had to be cut down for all of us to receive just about every material possession we own. Whether it's microwaves, fridge freezers, cookers, heaters, the glass in our windows, the wood around our house, the bricks that build our house, the asphalt that makes our road, and the phones that we all use.

At one point, lots of beautiful scenery was cut down so we could have what we have now. Lots of animals and insects lost their homes and were killed. And Lord only knows how many millions of worms have died at the hands of humans who were building something.

Do I feel bad about it, fuck no! Should you feel bad about it? Hell no!

Imagine what your life would be like every time you turned on your TV or made a phone call and you thought about how many innocent woodland creatures had to die because you have your phone. It would drive you insane!

My friend that sent me the photos of Hong Kong is a wonderful human being. He is kind and generous and I have to say he's one of my best friends. But there are also times when I have told him he has to toughen the fuck up for his own sake.

I'm not always that blunt with him. However, I will point out the benefits that he has received along with billions of other people because of technology and industry.

Sometimes he will quietly say back to me,

"I know Mark, but it's terrible, isn't it? I just wish things weren't like this."

The reality of life is that's the way things are and there's nothing you or I could do to change it. And if someone tried to grind industry to a halt and made everyone live in the woods, I'm sure the shit will hit the fan in every nation!

My father is similar. Again, he is a kind soul, but whenever I visit him, he likes to talk about global warming and tells me about the latest thing David Attenborough is saying.

I totally get it. If we can make the environment cleaner, breathe better air and provide a better future for our children, I'm all in with that. And don't get me wrong here, I'm a big fan of the documentaries David Attenborough has done.

However, on a personal level. Would I stop driving my car to help the environment? Can't say I would. Will I stop travelling to places around the world and stop taking my son Léon to awesome destinations on planes, trains, and automobiles to help the environment? I think not! Rightly or wrongly, my number one priority is to help create the best life I can for my son. If you have a similar priority, you will think the same way.

However, if somebody wants to live in the wilderness to help the environment, crack on!

Every convenience we have is created by industry and there is always going to be a cost to the environment for products now considered essential to human beings.

I think David Attenborough is cool and if he can draw attention to some issues that make a difference, great! David Attenborough has made almost 400 trips to 94 countries and has pumped more ozone smashing fuel into the atmosphere than 99.9% of individuals. He has one of the biggest carbon footprints in history so many will not listen to him for obvious reasons.

Will I stop using phones, laptops, transportation, books, and everything else that improves my life because of collateral damage? I'll pass on that one.

The world is tough enough without you making it harder for yourself. It's great to care about the environment and animals. However, if you become an emotional basket-case because you want nothing to die, you'll mash your brain up!

There are some things you'll be able to change and some things that you can't change. There are also things that you shouldn't change and providing the best life for yourself and your family is one of those things. So, if you are doing so, toughen up and stop looking for all the faults of the human race. If you're already good with this, brilliant!

CHAPTER 12

TERRIBLE START TO TERRIFIC TRIUMPH

"You are under no obligation to remain the same person you were a year ago, a month ago, or even a day ago. You are here to create yourself continuously."
– Richard Feynman

I can't tell you how many times I've failed in life because it's such a large number, but I can tell you how many times I've got back up. Every single time! And that's all you need to do. Yes, it's easier said than done, but it can be done.

When legendary comedian Steve Martin started comedy, he was in a club called 'The Icehouse.' About halfway through Steve's 25-minute show, he realised he didn't get one laugh from the crowd.

Rather than be discouraged, Steve adapted and set a new goal, which was to get 25 minutes with no laughter at all. This may seem like an unusual goal; however, it was done for an exceptionally good reason. He knew that night was probably going to be the worst night he would have and thought things could only get better from then on.

This is a brilliant way to interpret a failure. Steve knew that even if he got a smile out of the crowd on his second performance, it would be an improvement. He knew if he could get one chuckle on his third performance, he was making progress.

In Steve Martin's early days as a comedian, he always went on stage filled with anxiety and was getting heart palpitations. He also got panic attacks and thought he was going to die. One day, Steve ended up in hospital. However, despite such knock-backs, Steve persisted and never gave in!

Although Steve Martin became a hugely successful comedian, things didn't always go his way. A part of his act was for his guitar to be lowered down from the ceiling and given to him. However, for several nights in a row there were technical problems, and it didn't come down. That could've thrown some people, but Steve soldiered on.

When Steve started out, he faked his confidence. He knew before he went on stage, he was nervous, but acted as if he wasn't nervous. The more he acted like he wasn't nervous, the more confident he became and was later comfortable on stage in front of thousands of people.

I know from personal experience, when you're on stage and you're confident, you don't care what people think. When you're like that, no negative person in the audience can rock you. What's important is that your confidence relaxes them. If you look like a bag of nerves, the audience can feel it, which can often make them feel nervous for you.

One day while Steve was performing on stage, a guy threw a glass of wine over him. This was only one challenge he went through, but he never gave up. This mental toughness led him to the success he would later achieve.

When I produce my books, I almost always put a quote from somebody at the start of the chapter. With this chapter, I came across Richard Feynman's quote and thought that it matched the chapter perfectly. However, as much as I liked the quote, I didn't know who Richard Feynman was, so I did some research on him. The last thing I want to do, is not research the person and put a quote in my book that belongs to a paedo or a serial killer. So, you'll be reassured to know that there are no quotes in my books from Jimmy Savile, Jeffrey Epstein, Dr Harold Shipman, Ted Bundy, or Adolf Hitler.

But all jokes aside, the more I read about Richard Feynman, the more impressed I was with his story. Richard was a late talker and did not speak a word until well after his third birthday. He was influenced by his dad, who encouraged him to challenge orthodox thinking and his dad always taught him something new.

Even though Richard started off slow and his parents were worried about his lack of progress as a small child, at 15 he taught himself trigonometry, infinite series, advanced algebra, analytic geometry, and integral calculus.

In his last year of high school, Richard won the New York University maths championship.

He applied to get into Columbia University but was rejected because of the number of Jews that were admitted. Although this was disheartening, he stayed strong and applied to get into the Massachusetts Institute of Technology, otherwise known as MIT. With an acceptance rate of only 7% the odds were against him.

However, he was bold, he studied hard and was later accepted.

Richard received his bachelor's degree and also had a perfect score on the graduate school entrance exams for Princeton University in physics. This was another outstanding achievement from the boy that started slowly in life!

He went on to work at Cornell and the California Institute of Technology (AKA Cal Tech).

Richard became a master in quantum electrodynamics

and quantum mechanics. He's a recipient of the Albert Einstein Award Medal, The National Medal of Science and the Nobel Prize in Physics for his fundamental work in quantum electrodynamics.

Many people would've written Richard off with achieving anything because of his slow start in life. But a tough start in life can often be a great foundation to achieving enormous success!

Steve Martin and Richard Feynman knew that just because they had failed in their early days, they didn't have to become failures in life. When they got knocked back, they knew it was time to toughen up and work harder than ever before!

Just because you've had a terrible start it doesn't mean that you will end up failing. The only way you can fail is if you give up after the first failure. And it can often be if you give up too soon. Maybe you failed 10, 20 or 50 times, but what if that breakthrough that you were looking for was on the 51st time? You never know when your breakthrough is going to come, so you have to keep on persisting and moving forward!

If you ever started an exercise routine, you'll know you weren't great at the start. Yes, you could've been given a natural amount of fitness or strength, however even after only 30 days of training you would see a dramatic improvement in your strength and fitness.

If you're overweight and you haven't got that six pack or flat tummy after a week, a month, or three months of training, it doesn't mean you should give up. However, what you should do is look for minor improvements every day. There will be days and weeks where you may not see an improvement in your fitness, strength, or weight loss.

When this happens, analyse what you have been eating and also look carefully at your training program. Chances are, there will be some tweaks you can make to get better results. If you're struggling to get results as fast as you would like, it may be time to get a friend to train with, or even a fitness professional such as a personal trainer, or a nutritionist. Getting help from somebody can have a dramatic impact on your results!

A recent example of this for myself is my friend and colleague Tom Webb who helps with many aspects of my publishing business. As a self-published author you have to do not only the writing, but you also have to know the publishing and marketing side of things as well. There are a huge number of things to learn and do. I got to the stage where I realised I wasn't producing as many books as I wanted to, so I needed to get someone else in to help me.

Tom initially came on board as my cover designer. After he succeeded with my cover designs, I asked him if he could help with the formatting. He wasn't an expert at formatting to start off, but he is very intelligent and learnt how to do it quickly. I needed more help and wondered what else Tom could master, so in 2021, I introduced Tom to other aspects of publishing. By doing this, I could concentrate on my writing. As I write this book, Tom is now learning about the marketing side of publishing, so I can concentrate on my writing more. I will still always be involved with the marketing side, however two brains are better than one and you will move forward far quicker with somebody else's help, knowledge, and support.

We both know that I got off to a slow start as an author, but we also realise that becoming a successful author is like putting a gigantic jigsaw puzzle together. At the start you only have one piece, but every time you make an improvement, you're adding another jigsaw piece to your puzzle.

If you've got a big enough reason to achieve what you want to achieve and you are persistent, chances are you're going to succeed in a big way!

You just have to keep moving forward, one step at a time and adding one jigsaw piece to the puzzle every day. So, no matter how slowly you start, or how many times you fail, always pick yourself back up and keep moving forward towards your goal!

CHAPTER 13

RECOVERING FROM MISTAKES

"Mistakes are part of being human. Appreciate your mistakes for what they are: precious life lessons that can only be learnt the hard way. Unless it's a fatal mistake, which, at least, others can learn from."

– Al Franken

Mentally tough people recover from setbacks quicker than the average person. They view setbacks as part of life's little game and don't let setbacks and mistakes stop them from achieving their goals.

Strong-minded people know there is usually something good that comes from setbacks. And they know they can always learn from their mistakes.

In 2016, I interviewed explorer Levison Wood. I contacted him through Twitter and met him at his house in London.

Lev, as he likes to be called, is a former British Army officer who served with the Parachute Regiment as a Captain and was involved in Operation Herrick in Afghanistan.

In 2010 he left the army and started a new career as a writer and a photographer. He has travelled to over 100 countries and in 2011 was made a fellow of the Royal Geographical Society. He is an elected fellow of the

Explorers Club in New York and he holds an honorary doctorate at Staffordshire University.

Lev is best known for his documentaries, 'Walking the Nile,' 'Walking the Himalayas: An Adventure of Survival and Endurance,' 'Walking the America's' and 'Incredible Journeys: Discovery, Adventure, Danger, Endurance.'

While I was interviewing Lev, some people walked into the room and disrupted the interview. No big deal, I could always edit that bit out. Apart from that, it was a brilliant interview, and we both enjoyed our chat.

Back then, I recorded many of my interviews on my phone and the interview with Lev was the first time I recorded an interview using 4K resolution. And I was excited to see how good it looked.

When we finished the interview, I checked my phone to see the footage and my heart sank. Out of the 17-minute interview, it only recorded 5 minutes. The rest of the interview was lost! There was only one word that flashed through my mind.

"Fuck!"

I had completely balls'd things up. How embarrassing.

I had two choices. I could either tell Lev it went perfectly, or I could tell him the truth and say I'd wasted a load of time because the camera wasn't even recording.

I thought if I told him the truth, he may take it badly and say something like, "Look I haven't got time for this and I'm not doing another one."

However, I believed that telling him the truth was the right thing to do, even though I knew it might upset him. I explained what had happened and waited for him to say something.

There was a pause, and a deathly silence in the room! You know the type. It's like when a stranger walks into a bar in a western movie. The people in the bar all go quiet and the music stops playing. It was as if I could hear the cogs ticking away in Lev's mind, and I wondered if he would blow a gasket!

Although I had made a stupid blunder, and I felt a little embarrassed, at the same time there was a bit of excitement in me. I wanted to see how he handled the situation. I wanted to see if Lev would go ape-shit and throw his teddy in the corner. He looks cool on TV, but let's see how he reacts when the cameras aren't rolling.

I worked as a bouncer for nine years. Although I enjoyed

evenings where there was no fighting, I also got excited when all hell broke loose in the nightclubs! After all, no cowboy movie is complete without a bar-fight scene.

I was incredibly lucky in those nine years because I never got severely hurt. I never even got beat up. However, there was a lot of luck in that. All it would've taken was the wrong night, against the wrong person, or against the wrong people.

I know many people who have completed tough endurance challenges, but they lose their shit over the silliest thing. The people that I've always admired the most are the people that keep calm in real-life situations.

When somebody loses their temper, they are acting from a low level of consciousness. If you are one of these people, you've got to get past this. Not only can losing your temper make you look like a bit of a dick, but you also lose your ability to think rationally when that angry red mist has set in. If this happens, you can lose valuable relationships and have a lot more regrets. Losing your temper can even land you in prison, so being able to keep calm when challenges come your way is vital in life!

Lev could have acted like a spoilt diva and lost his cool. After a few seconds in deep thought, he looked at the wall opposite him, and waved his hand as if to gesture us moving forward.

He said,

"No worries, we can do it again."

It was in that moment that my respect for Lev became greater than ever before. Sure, he had achieved some impressive things in life, but more importantly, he was polite and kept his cool.

Although there was that devil in me waiting to see how he reacted, there is also a part of me where I care about other people. When I meet people, I don't try to upset them, I just want them to have an enjoyable experience.

Because I have these two types of mindsets, I have set myself up to win in either situation. And you can do the same thing.

If things go well, brilliant! If things don't go so well, brilliant!

You can learn from your mistakes and take the positives out of that experience.

Because I had made mistakes, it gave me the opportunity

to write about it in this book. Had that first interview gone well, I wouldn't have written about it, because the behind-the-scenes back story of that interview wasn't as interesting.

As we started 'Take 2,' I messed up the introduction, stopped the interview and said to Lev,

"We'll do that again if that's ok?"

Again, to his credit, Lev took it in his stride and said,

"No problem, I've done loads of this type of stuff and these things happen."

This made me feel a little better, but I knew I had to forget about my blunders, stay positive and keep the interview moving on a positive note.

While going through the interview, I doubted if it would be as good as the first interview because I had ruined the atmosphere a little. Nevertheless, I ploughed through the interview, smiling, and joking.

After the initial disappointment, we got there in the end. For the next few hours, I was a little pissed off with myself and sent the interview to my mate Matt Dix. Matt is great at giving feedback. He is the type of person who will tell me what he thinks, rather than just what I want to hear.

Matt said the interview was brilliant, and after looking at it, I thought, 'yeah that's rather good.' Things can often seem worse in the moment than they are when you look back at them.

You can see the interview if you type in my name and Lev's name on YouTube.

If you're a human being, you're going to make mistakes. That's the way it is, and everybody makes them. The most important thing to remember is to keep your cool during challenging times and keep moving forward towards your goals!

If you keep on replaying your mistakes, the tragedies that you've been and your setbacks… your life is going to be pretty shit!

Wow, that's blunt, isn't it? But I'm here to give you the truth and not mollycoddle you. If you already have a certain amount of mental toughness, you will take on board those words and move forward.

After you have made mistakes, it's vital that you don't beat yourself up about them and keep on replaying them in your mind. You must override your negative thoughts with positive thoughts. This isn’t always a simple thing to do, but it can be done!

You were born with phenomenal inner strength. It’s always there, sometimes we just forget it’s there. So, tap back into your inner strength and live that incredible life that you deserve to live!

CHAPTER 14

PURPOSE AND COURAGE

"Courage is being scared to death…
and saddling up anyway."
– John Wayne

There will be times in your life when you need to toughen up and take risks. If your reason to take on risks is big enough, then take them on. If you don't, you could live the rest of your life with regrets, and nobody wants that.

If you don't toughen up, the consequences of not taking risks can be anything from bad to catastrophic!

In my book, 'Put Your Big Boy Pants On,' I wrote about the honey badger which is regarded by Guinness World Records as, 'The Most Fearless Animal in the World.' Taking on snakes, scorpions, and killer bees is all in a days work for the honey badger. That's just how it rolls!

However, in this chapter, you will read about another creature that is not universally known for its courage. In fact, if a human got into a rumble with one, you'd be certain you could easily defeat it. However, if I asked you who would win out of a human and a polar bear in hand to paw battle, I think we all know what your answer would be. This next story illustrates the bravery and toughness of this common, but remarkable creature.

I visited my mum one day, and she was watching a documentary on the Arctic which showed a hungry polar bear looking for some food. The polar bear had found some birds' eggs, but it was looking for something a little more substantial and came into an area where there was a young chick.

The young seagull chick knew it was in danger, so it hid behind a rock and released a couple of cries for help.

The polar bear started walking to the rock that the chick was hiding behind. At this point in the documentary, death for the young chick looked inevitable! However, all hope was not lost.

Mummy and daddy seagulls heard the cries of their young chick. Within seconds, they had put their big bird pants on, and descended on the Arctic's most feared predator. They not only dive bombed the polar bear to distract it from the cries of the chick, but they also struck the polar bear with their beaks and drew blood from its sensitive nose area.

It was like watching the equivalent of a human bobbing up and down on a bungee cord and fighting a T-Rex with a toothpick. I've seen a lot of cool movies involving aeroplanes in dogfights. However, I've never seen such an impressive aerial attack as this mummy and daddy seagull launched on the killer polar bear.

Amazingly, the polar bear retreated and walked off in the opposite direction from the young chick.

Who would've thought that two tiny birds could've inflicted this sort of damage on a polar bear? Of course, they risked their own lives by dive bombing the polar bear, but they were were willing to take on that risk.

If you're a parent, or you have a loved one, and would put your own life in danger to protect them, you'll know what I mean when I write, 'If the purpose is significant enough, the facts don't count.' No matter what the odds are against you, you're going to do everything humanly possible to save your loved one!

When the polar bear was about to kill their chick, the seagull's major purpose was to save their baby, no matter what the odds were, or the danger they put themselves in. Who would've believed that these little birds would've beaten a polar bear but beat the polar bear they did!

I tried to find the article or a video of this extraordinary event so I could credit the cameraman, production company and the TV channel involved. Unfortunately, I couldn't find a video or an article on it. However, I came across another article in the Daily Mail about another courageous seagull having a fight with a polar bear. But in this polar bear attack, the seagull wasn't fighting to save the life of another, it was fighting for its own life!

On 28 of December 2010, an article was published online in the Daily Mail about a seagull being attacked by the polar bear. However, this wasn't an aerial bombardment by the seagull like the previous story. This was a full-on, one-on-one land battle. Now, you would think a land battle with a polar bear and a seagull would be over within the first few seconds. However, it lasted several minutes. And the amazing thing about this land attack that made it even more mind blowing was, the seagull won the battle!

Photographer Ole Jorgen Liodden was taking photos of a seagull minding its own business in the water. Without the seagull knowing it, a polar bear entered the water and sneakily swam up to the unsuspecting seagull. Polar bears often kill seals and whales so you would think that killing a seagull from behind would be an easy meal for the polar bear. However, you'd be wrong.

The polar bear swam behind the seagull and clamped its powerful jaws into the seagull's back. Startled from this seagull sucker-punch, the seagull knew it had to fight for its life… and it would not give in without a fight!

The seagull turned around and landed some beak blows into the bear's sensitive nose and eyes. Stunned by this comeback of comebacks, the polar bear backed off and the seagull flew off into the sunset. But before the seagull flew off into the sunset, it circled the polar bear and shat on its head.

Okay, I don't know if it flew off into the sunset or if it took a dump on the polar bear's head, but it flew off. However, if I was writing a movie script, that's exactly what would've happened. I would've also added a scene with the seagull giving the polar bear its middle finger (if it had one), and another scene where the seagull says to the polar bear, "How do you like them apples!"

Unfortunately, those things only happen in the movies.

Back in the real world, with these two attacks, the birds didn't give a hoot about how big and deadly the polar bear was. In the first story, the seagull's goal was to save their baby chick's life, and they put their own lives on the line to save their baby. And in the second story, one seagull was fighting for its own life.

Hopefully, you'll never be in a position where you are being physically attacked and you are fighting for your life. And hopefully, you're never in a situation where your loved one's life is in mortal danger and you have to put your own life on the line to save your loved one.

The point of this chapter is, if your reason for being courageous and fighting is big enough, then it's worth doing. Everybody's reasons will be different. You may want to provide the best life for yourself or your family, but you must make some bold moves to make your dreams come true. Maybe there are some big personal goals that you want to set for yourself. The odds look like they are staggeringly against you, and maybe nobody believes in you, but that's exactly when it's time to toughen up.

You must go out of your comfort zone and you must toughen up to achieve your goals. So, focus on your reason for doing what you want to do and think about the benefits it will provide you and others if you accomplish your goal. Life is too short to not take any chances.

You can just sit on the sidelines like many critics do and just talk about other people's crazy dreams and failures and successes. Or you can be inspired by other people who have achieved great things in their lives, and you can make your own dreams come true. It takes a lot of bravery to achieve your goals, but they can be achieved.

So, it's time to toughen up and just go for it!

ACKNOWLEDGEMENTS

It's almost impossible to say how many people have helped me along the way with producing this book, and if you're not in the acknowledgements just know that I am very grateful for your support and help.

However, I would like to say a massive THANK YOU to a few people that I can think of, off the top of my head:

Tracy and Kay Morris, Tom Webb, Paul 'The Viking' Hughes, Thomas Hughes, Eva Savage, Mark 'Billy' Billingham, Julie Colombino-Billingham, Cheryl Hicks, Jamie Baulch, Gene Hipgrave, Mark Dawson, Craig Martelle, Michael Anderle, James Blatch, Michael and Emma Byrne, Paul 'Faz' Farrington, Paul Heaney, James Atkinson, Des Powell and Laura Taylor.

Big thanks to 29 Commando Regiment, Royal Artillery, 3 Commando Brigade and The British Army.

Also, a huge THANKS to 'The Mark Llewhellin Advance Reader Team' for taking the time to read the manuscript and make suggestions.

ABOUT THE AUTHOR

In 1990, Mark Llewhellin left school without knowing his grades. He had little confidence and was not at all optimistic about his future.

Not knowing what to do with his life Mark followed some of his friends into the Army. He failed his basic 1.5-mile run, was bullied, and was also voted the fattest person in the Troop!

After a year with the Junior Leaders Regiment Royal Artillery, Mark decided he would try and get into 29 Commando Regiment Royal Artillery, which is an elite Army Commando Regiment that at the time proudly held the Military Marathon World Record (i.e. a marathon carrying a 40lbs backpack).

After failing the 29 Commando Selection phase (called 'The Beat Up') twice, first through lack of fitness and secondly through an injury, Mark subsequently passed on his third attempt and completed the 'All Arms Commando Course' on his first attempt.

Mark later went on to achieve the following:

- Break the 100-kilometre Treadmill World Record.

- Place 1st in the Strava Distance Challenge in 2015 competing against over 51,000 runners.

- Place 1st in the Strava Distance Challenge in 2014 competing against over 40,000 runners.

- Run and walk 70-miles without training on his 40th birthday.

- Become a successful Personal Fitness Trainer.

- Complete the Marathon Des Sables (a six-day, 135-mile ultra-marathon in the Sahara Desert).

- Work and live in London's exclusive Park Lane as a Bodyguard.

- Run 1,620 miles in the United States whilst carrying a 35lbs pack.

Mark has interviewed some of the world's top performers and high achievers in various locations, including one of the world's most prestigious memorabilia rooms…the Hard Rock Café Vault Room in London.

He has travelled to over 50 countries and has been featured in leading national newspapers and on TV for his running achievements.

Mark has extensively worked in the support and care industry for many years helping individuals with brain injury, autism, epilepsy, dyspraxia, and various types of learning difficulties.

He is the Managing Director of Mark 7 Productions, as well as the Producer and Host of 'An Audience with Mark Billy Billingham' speaking events around the UK.

Mark is currently working on more personal development books and lives with his son Léon (when Léon's not at his Mum's) on a beautiful marina in South West Wales.

ALSO BY MARK LLEWHELLIN

"Powerful. A must read!"
Mark 'Billy' Billingham – TV's Most Highly Decorated SAS Leader
MAN THE F*CK UP
HOW TO PICK YOURSELF UP AND SUCCEED WHEN LIFE BITCH SLAPS YOU
MARK LLEWHELLIN

NUMBER 1 BESTSELLING AUTHOR
SMUG BASTARD
DEVELOP UNSTOPPABLE SELF CONFIDENCE
AND GO SCREAMING PAST PEOPLE THAT HATE YOUR GUTS
MARK LLEWHELLIN

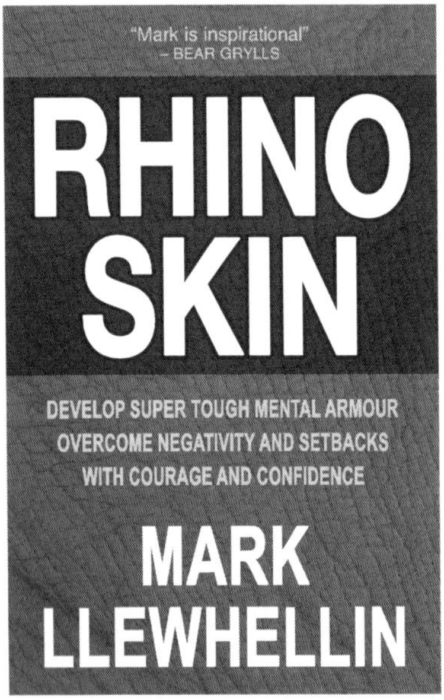
"Mark is inspirational"
– BEAR GRYLLS
RHINO SKIN
DEVELOP SUPER TOUGH MENTAL ARMOUR
OVERCOME NEGATIVITY AND SETBACKS
WITH COURAGE AND CONFIDENCE
MARK LLEWHELLIN

NUMBER 1 BESTSELLING AUTHOR
STAY STRONG
ELIMINATE NEGATIVE THINKING AND BECOME
A STRONGER AND MORE POSITIVE PERSON
MARK LLEWHELLIN

"POWERFUL!"
Kate Strong – World Triathlon Champion
PUT YOUR BIG BOY PANTS ON
HOW TO MASTER YOUR MIND AND EMOTIONS
BUILD SUPERIOR MENTAL TOUGHNESS
THINK POSITIVE AND LIVE THE GOOD LIFE
MARK LLEWHELLIN

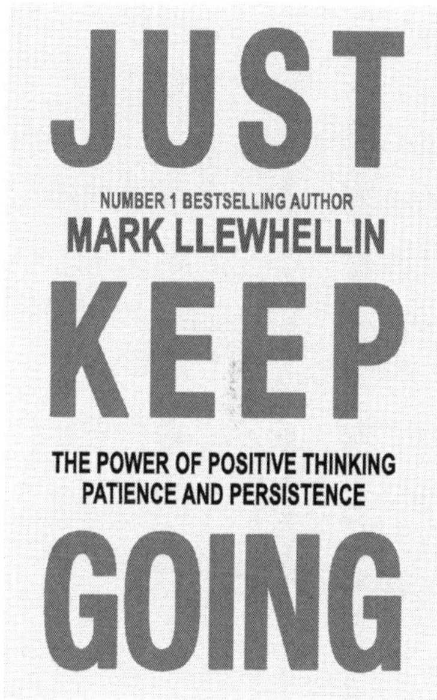
JUST
NUMBER 1 BESTSELLING AUTHOR
MARK LLEWHELLIN
KEEP
THE POWER OF POSITIVE THINKING
PATIENCE AND PERSISTENCE
GOING

AN EASY GUIDE TO ACHIEVING YOUR GOALS
AND TRANSFORMING YOUR LIFE
JUST GO FOR IT
NUMBER 1 BESTSELLING AUTHOR
MARK LLEWHELLIN

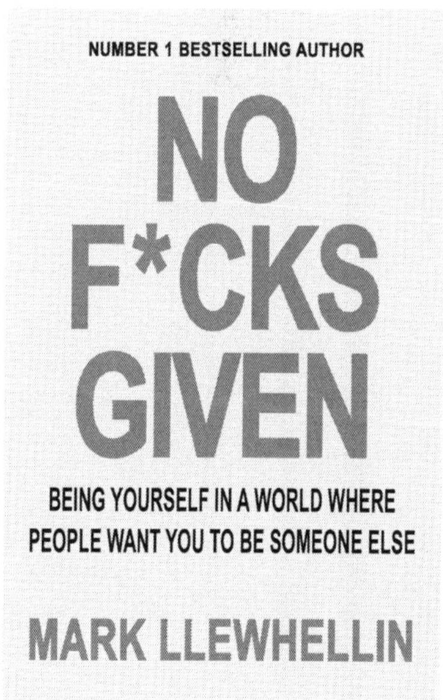
NUMBER 1 BESTSELLING AUTHOR
NO F*CKS GIVEN
BEING YOURSELF IN A WORLD WHERE
PEOPLE WANT YOU TO BE SOMEONE ELSE
MARK LLEWHELLIN

GET TWO FREE MARK LLEWHELLIN BOOKS AND DEALS AND UPDATES

Join 'The Mark Llewhellin Advance Reader Team' for information on new books and deals plus:

You can pick up FREE copies of Mark's five star reviewed books:

1. 'The Underdog'

2. 'Delusions of Grandeur'

Simply go to Mark's website at www.markllewhellin.com and sign up for FREE.

REFERENCES

National History Museum
Oprah Winfrey
Jonathan Ross
VYBO
Skavlan
Killahh Bee
Comedians in Cars Getting Coffee
Wikipedia
Ranker
Nick Llubichich – Nick12x2
Deep Marine Scenes
People
Amazon Prime
The Fantasy Makers: Tolkien, Lewis, and McDonald

DISCLAIMER

Although the author and publisher have made every effort to ensure that the information contained in this book was accurate at the time of release, the author and publisher do not assume and hereby disclaim any liability to any party for any loss, damage, or disruption caused by errors or omissions in this book, whether such errors or omissions result from negligence, accident, or any other cause.

A Mark 7 Publications Paperback.

First published in Great Britain in 2021

by Mark 7 Publications

ISBN 978-1-914006-58-6

Book design and formatting by Tom Webb
pixelfiddler@hotmail.co.uk

IF YOU ENJOYED THIS BOOK

Your help in spreading the word about Mark's books is greatly appreciated and your reviews make a huge difference to help new readers change their lives for the better.

If you found this book useful please leave a review on the platform you purchased it on.

Live Your Dreams!

Mark

Printed in Great Britain
by Amazon

73049784R00092